CULTURAL FUSION
QUILTS

A Melting Pot of Piecing Traditions

15 Free-Form Block Projects

Sujata Shah

PUBLISHING

Publisher: Amy Marson

Creative Director: Gailen Runge

Art Director: Kristy Zacharias

Editor: Deb Rowden

Technical Editors: Teresa Stroin and Debbie Rodgers

Cover Designer: April Mostek

Book Designer: Christina Jarumay Fox

Production Coordinator: Rue Flaherty

Production Editor: Alice Mace Nakanishi

Illustrator: Wendy Mathson

Photo Assistant: Mary Peyton Peppo

Style photography by Nissa Brehmer and instructional photography by Diane Pedersen, unless otherwise noted

Published by C&T Publishing, Inc., P.O. Box 1456, Lafayette, CA 94549

Library of Congress Cataloging-in-Publication Data

Shah, Sujata, 1963-

Cultural fusion quilts : a melting pot of piecing traditions : 15 free-form block projects / Sujata Shah.

    pages cm

Includes bibliographical references and index.

ISBN 978-1-60705-809-0 (soft cover : alk. paper)

1. Patchwork quilts. 2. Patchwork--Patterns. 3. Quilting--Patterns. I. Title.

TT835.S46285 2014

746.46--dc23

                          2014009335

Printed in China

10 9 8 7 6 5 4 3 2 1

DEDICATION

To my father, Jagmohandas Gandhi, and my mother, Saudamini Gandhi.

My father taught me to feel the dirt in my toes and smell the flowers. Without him, I wouldn't know to be authentic and true to my soul and surroundings.

My mother showed me to be curious and creative, improvise, and embrace life to its fullest. Without her exuberance, I wouldn't know to appreciate little things that matter the most.

ACKNOWLEDGMENTS

This book would have remained a dream if it weren't for contributions of many friends and family members around the world.

I would like to thank my husband, Nilesh, for being a constant and positive voice in my head, insisting that I follow my heart. My kids—Gautam, Shail, and Kavita—are the reason I took on sewing as a hobby. Gautam's curiosity about why I was sewing only with strips created a shift in my thought process. Shail's interest and care for what I do has existed since he was a little boy. My daughter Kavita's soulful and earthy personality makes me look at the world with a different eye. This project could not have been completed without her patience and willingness to help every step of the way.

Dorothy (Sally) LeBeouf, LeeAnn Decker, Helen Knopf, Mary Keasler, Kelly Meanix, and Christine Kamon made quilts for the book. Always just a phone call away, they had words of wisdom that have been like a cozy quilt on a cold rainy day in Seattle. Quilts for this book would never have been completed if it were not for Barbara Jackson's timely machine quilting service. Thanks to the Quiltinis for continuous encouragement and laughter since the first day I met them. Rose Burkette, Myra Mitchell, and Barbara Fiddes were the first few friends who recognized I had something to offer to the quilting community in Seattle. I am sincerely thankful for the teaching opportunities provided by Liz Warner and Stacie Baumeister and students who dove right into every challenge I presented when I was finding my own voice.

I am grateful for the enthusiasm shared by family members in Pennsylvania. My sisters Kalpana and Vandana's trust in me made it possible to self-appoint as a designer at a very young age. Ashish Shah has readily and willingly helped me through any and all computer crises I have encountered through this process.

My deepest gratitude goes to Barbara Brackman for the vote of confidence and encouragement at the beginning of this adventure. Thanks to my editor, Deb Rowden, I now know a little about writing a book.

CONTENTS

INTRODUCTION 4

MY JOURNEY AS A QUILTER 5

FREE-FORM BLOCKS 9

FABRIC SELECTION 17

THE QUILTS

Crazy Quilt 19

Rail Fence 24

Toran 30

Hourglass Baby Quilt 35

Hourglass Twist 40

Windmills 46

Rocky Road to Kansas 50

Lattice 55

Crossroads 59

Square in a Square 64

Sunset 68

Zigzag Amish Impressions 74

Peppermint Pinwheels 79

Endless Mountains 83

Winter 90

ABOUT THE AUTHOR 95

INTRODUCTION

Sujata Shah has a wonderful eye. We've never met in person, but we have been Internet pals for several years. Somehow, through friends of friends, we wound up together in a rebellious online quilting group. I marvel at their ways of looking at the world.

And of course, with Sujata we actually get a world perspective. How lucky we are to look over her shoulder as she puts her colorful spin on everything she sees, absorbs, and interprets. Ideas bounce from Gee's Bend, Alabama, to India by way of Philadelphia thrift shops and back into her studio.

As a quilt historian, I've always looked at the American quilt as a recipe for our melting pot, beginning with a stew of English bedding traditions, Dutch fondness for fabrics traded from around the world, German folk design, and French provincial prints. India's fabrics have long been in the mix—with actual yardage imported through the India trade; design and technology borrowed for classic calico; and chintz industrialized by European mills.

Sujata, a professional designer raised in the colorful textile landscape of India, is in a unique position to add to the quilt's recipe for the twenty-first century. Deb Rowden, her editor here, and I are both privileged to know her and her quilts. Through this book we have encouraged Sujata to introduce herself to you. But let's let her tell her story. She does it so well in her words and her work.

—*Barbara Brackman*

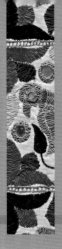

MY JOURNEY AS A QUILTER

 I grew up in India, a country well known for its textiles and colors. From traditional clothing to festive decorations, bold and vibrant textiles were part of my daily life.

In those days, our clothes were sewn at home or custom made by tailors. My mother recognized my love for fabrics. I would accompany her to the markets and select the fabrics for our clothes.

As much as I loved selecting fabric, I wasn't a bit interested in stitching. The entire process was tedious and boring to me. I remember telling my mother, "I would rather die than hold a needle in my hand."

I went to art school to study graphic design, where I developed an eye for patterns and textures. I drew inspirations from folk art and crafts. When I arrived in the United States in 1986 as a newlywed bride, clean lines and soft, muted gray tones greeted me at the airport. I was like a character from a color film that had walked into a black-and-white film. For a native of the tropics, I was always cold in San Francisco. I felt clumsy wearing brightly colored Indian outfits that were halfway covered with a mismatched gray coat. In an effort to blend in, I neatly packed away my saris for occasional use and adopted the lifestyle of the West.

Hand-embroidered wallhanging, Gujarat, India

Photo by Sujata Shah

A street vendor selling saris, India

In the early 1990s, I discovered handmade dolls at a local craft show. They reminded me of puppets from Rajasthan, India. With spare time on my hands and needing to be creative, I started making dolls. I often wondered about their purpose, but I couldn't stop making them. It was too much fun to design their outfits and give them personalities.

Puppets made from wood and cloth, India

Trips to the fabric shop led to a basic quiltmaking class. Watching quilt blocks evolve from geometric-shaped pieces of fabrics was like looking at a kaleidoscope changing patterns with every twist and turn. For the first time in my life, I was designing with fabric, sewing, and feeling good about it.

First quilt, pieced and hand quilted by Sujata Shah, 1992

My husband's career took us to Seattle, Washington, where I would grow as a quilter. A new friend reintroduced me to quilting. Inspired by her work, I pulled out my first quilt to finish the hand quilting. Every stitch reminded me of my teen years in India and my mother's enthusiasm about embroidery and sewing. In 1998, I hand appliquéd and hand quilted a bed-size quilt for my mother. It was a project we both will never forget. I was back in the world of textiles, colors, and textures—this time with a newer canvas and a larger palette. The teenage girl who was never going to sew was not only designing quilt patterns but also teaching at a local quilt shop.

In 2002–2003, my perspective on quilting changed when I discovered books about the quilts of Gee's Bend, Alabama, and ralli quilts from India. Although the quilts from these two locales are contrasting in appearance, conceptually there is a striking resemblance between them and also between the lives of the women who made them. The women of both cultures drew inspiration from their surroundings and spilled their souls into utilitarian quilts. Ralli quilts from India and Pakistan, inspired by motifs seen on ancient architecture and pottery, resemble antique American folk art and Amish quilts.

A light bulb went on! The two cultures blended instantly in my brain, which had become a melting pot of images of architecture, quilts, textiles, and crafts from India and Africa. Irregularities and imperfections in block prints from India, mud and raffia cloth, and handmade crafts of Africa became the driving force behind my interpretations of traditional quilt blocks.

I wanted more than just straight lines in my quilts.

Appliqué ralli quilt, from Rajasthan, India, shown hanging in a window, maker unknown, author's collection

Balcony of a fort in Rajasthan, India

Block print, northwest India

Embroidered silk dress, eastern India

Ikat fabric, western India

Wood blocks for printing
borders and blocks on fabric, India

Handcrafted folk art birds,
southern India

FREE-FORM BLOCKS

AN ABSTRACT INTERPRETATION OF TRADITIONAL QUILT BLOCKS

After discovering the quilts of Gee's Bend, my focus shifted from traditional quilts to utilitarian and improvisational quilts. African-American quilts in books such as *Bold Improvisation* by Scott Heffley and *Accidentally on Purpose* by Eli Leon reminded me of *godharis*, utilitarian quilts from India. Quilts made with scraps on hand have a graphic and bold identity of their own.

The use of traditional quilt patterns made with nontraditional fabrics created unique movement and fluidity in this art form. These quilts became a huge source of inspiration for me and caused me to want organic lines in traditional quilt blocks.

In 2004, I made a quilt as a class sample to teach a workshop based on the quilts of Gee's Bend. Stacking squares of fabrics and cutting in layers allowed me to make multiple units of fabric strips. Each unit contained the same fabrics but with a different placement. Using scissors instead of a rotary cutter was a key factor in achieving the organic look of these quilts.

I continued experimenting with slicing gentle, curved strips and then swapping and sewing the pieces into a block. The next quilt I made was an interpretation of zebra cloth. All things African fascinated me, and this pattern was part of it. Stacks of two fabrics—hand cut in layers with scissors and simple lines—created an organic but somewhat organized look in the same quilt.

My first class sample—an abstract interpretation of a traditional nine-patch block

Zebra Quilt, 39½″ × 69½″, machine pieced and machine quilted by Sujata Shah, Chester Springs, Pennsylvania, 2006

The simplicity of the quilts of Gee's Bend and the graphic interpretation of traditional blocks in quilts made by other African-American quilters provided a unique blend of inspirations. I continued experimenting with lines—straight and diagonal—and with triangles and other patterns. I knew a new door of creativity had opened up for me.

A stack of two fabrics created a negative image of the block with inverted colors. The next obvious step was to add more fabrics to the stack. The relationship between using more fabrics and evolving patterns of blocks was an unstoppable and exciting process.

Negative-image blocks

Adding curves to the cutting process created a new design element. Quilts made with these curved blocks resembled the Gee's Bend quilts made with jersey material, cotton scraps on bias, and polyester and linen clothing. With a little pull here and a tug there, each quilt had its own identity. This process was freeing in more ways than I could imagine.

We know that each quilt reflects the personality of the maker. With each stack of free-form blocks, the personality of quilt blocks changes. Template-free cutting and a free piecing method create a perfect balance. They lend a modern twist to the organic and fluid nature of antique hand-pieced folk art quilts. They create white space and background. They also make shapes float and connect at surprising places. The results are always unpredictable.

What Inspires You?

Inspiration is different for everyone. Our nature and desire to create remain the same, but inspiration changes over time and life experiences. People we meet, places we travel, and sights we see all influence our creativity.

What inspires me is everything handmade. Irregularities, organic lines, disorganized shapes, and imperfections in handmade things make me wonder about the maker's life and mind-set during the making of the craft. I feel connected to my quilts because my life lives in them.

This book introduces a new way of interpreting the textures and patterns of handmade objects from our daily surroundings. Free-form blocks are nothing but a seed of an idea—like so many that have been planted for us to grow from. They are about exploring new possibilities and expanding creativity through organic piecing and quilting, while staying connected to traditional quilt patterns.

Exploring is about the process. The first step leads to the next: Curiosity and questions like, "What if?" and "How about?" take you to places you have never been before. Look at your surroundings. We gravitate to what makes us comfortable and happy. We gather what we like, and we grow from what we already know.

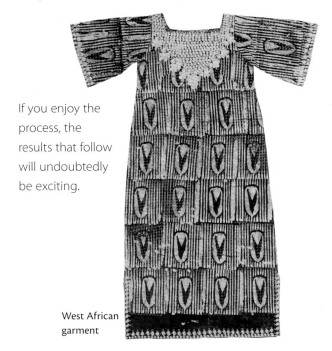

If you enjoy the process, the results that follow will undoubtedly be exciting.

West African garment

HOW TO MAKE FREE-FORM BLOCKS

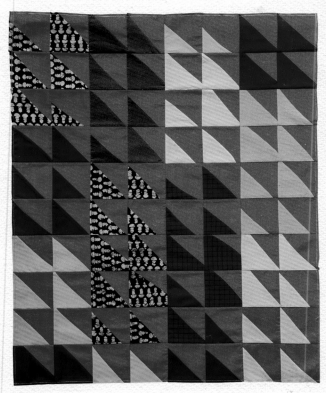

Floating triangles

Here are five simple steps for making free-form blocks.

1. Cut out squares from yardage.

2. With right sides up, stack the squares.

3. Cut through all the layers of the squares at once.

4. Slide the top layer of one section to the bottom of the same section to change the order of the sewing sequence.

5. Sew the blocks back together in the order they appear.

Unlike traditional blocks, this method gives you freedom to experiment with unusual sizes and shapes. Sewing curved pieces in this manner distorts the blocks. The top fabric always ends up extending beyond the bottom fabric after sewing. Don't worry—you'll square them up later.

START WITH SQUARES

Stack Squares Right Sides Up

When you use solid fabrics, mark the right side with a big X with a chalk marker until you get some practice keeping the sides straight.

How Many Squares Matters

The stack of squares should contain more than two fabrics. This guarantees blocks with no repeat color combinations. Try not to use the same fabric twice in a stack unless the pattern calls for it.

An odd number of squares in a stack can be tricky if you are looking for contrast in the patchwork. However, I recommend it for scrappy quilts. It provides unexpected results. An even number of squares in a stack helps to alternate value and colors.

Bond the Layers

To temporarily bond the layers, press the stack with a steam iron before cutting.

Keep a small, portable ironing board and a steam iron near your cutting table. Press the stack with full steam for just a few seconds. This is enough to bond the layers before cutting. This is a small step but quite helpful if you are a beginning quilter.

Cut the Layers

Note: Always cut away from you.

You can choose straight-line cutting or slight curves to cut the stacks. For straight cuts, use a ruler and rotary cutter to cut the layers. With either method, cut all the layers in the stack at once with a single stroke.

Keep the Rotary-Cutting Blade Sharp

Change blades in the rotary cutter frequently to make the cutting process easier.

While cutting gentle curves, use a ruler as a guide. Gently slide the ruler in the direction of the cut. You want to cut either a valley or a hill—but not both a hill and a valley in the same cut.

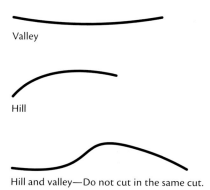

Valley

Hill

Hill and valley—Do not cut in the same cut.

Use the grids on the cutting mat as a general guide for the placement of the squares and cutting lines. You may be cutting freehand, but having some consistency in the cuts provides overall harmony in the quilt.

Sew the Block

Once the stack is sliced, you have pieces ready to sew. Be sure to sew them with right sides together.

Pinning is not required—the emphasis should be on imperfection and irregularities. I believe pins and markings create limitations while sewing the blocks.

Follow the step-by-step instructions in How to Sew Free-Form Blocks (page 13). With just a few practice blocks, you will be on your way to mastering this technique. Most of the imperfections can be steam-pressed and evened out or trimmed off at the end. Any puckering and unevenness remaining in the quilt top will disappear after quilting.

Chain Piecing

Chaining or chain piecing is the technique of sewing one similar unit after another without cutting the thread in between. It is sometimes referred to as assembly-line sewing and is very efficient. Chain piecing can speed the process along and help to avoid errors. It helps keep blocks in the right order. When sewing the second side of a block that has multiple cuts, cut loose only one unit at a time to avoid any mistakes in sewing order.

Press the Block

Free-form, curved piecing will distort the block. What started out as a perfect square will now look like a kite with tails at the end. Press the block using full steam with the iron. After the block is trimmed, avoid steam and only dry-press the blocks. Press down with an iron and lift up (an up-and-down motion), because ironing (a sliding motion) will distort the block.

Trim the Block

Trimming and squaring up free-form blocks is a fun process. This is when they start to become whimsical: Some lose tips, and some become lopsided. They even vary in size.

Press each block before trimming it. I prefer trimming each block individually to emphasize its wonkiness.

The size of each unfinished block will vary. The deeper the curves, the smaller the block will end up. Try not to make curves *too* deep. The goal is to create slight imperfection with a reasonable stretch of the fabric.

HOW TO SEW FREE-FORM BLOCKS

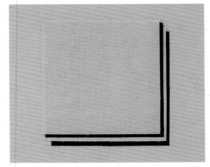

Stack of four, with two each of contrasting fabric squares

1. Start with a stack of 4 squares: 2 light and 2 dark.

2. Arrange them right sides up, alternating value and colors.

3. Align the squares corner to corner and edge to edge.

4. Before placing them on the cutting mat, steam-press to temporarily bond the stack.

5. With a rotary cutter, slice all the layers at once. Make the curve like either a hill or a valley (but not both in the same curve). Slowly slide the ruler slightly while cutting with a rotary cutter to achieve a gentle curve.

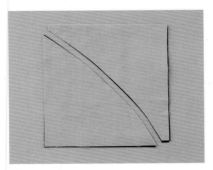

Slice a gentle curve.

 TIP

Replace or sharpen the rotary blade often. A dull blade will cause you to have to cut more than once and ruin the fluidity of the cut curve.

6. Keeping right sides up, slide the top layer of the right stack to the bottom of the right stack. This stack is now in the correct order for sewing the blocks.

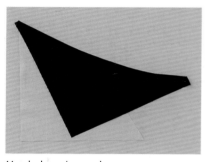

Slide.

7. With right sides together, match the starting points to start sewing the block. When sewn, the square will appear to have a tail, but this is normal.

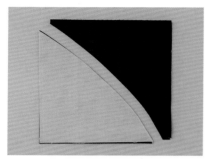

Match the points at the top.

8. Place the pieces with points matching under the presser foot. Stitch 4 to 6 stitches and pause.

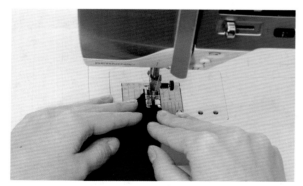

Stitch and pause.

9. Switch to holding the bottom piece with your right hand and the top piece with your left hand. Align the edges of the pieces as they feed into the machine.

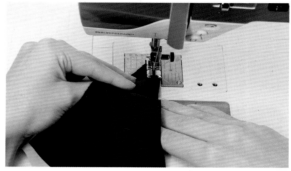

Guide pieces with both hands.

Lift the top layer if needed.

TIP

It helps to keep the edge of the bottom piece barely visible when sewing curves. It lets you see that you are stitching both layers.

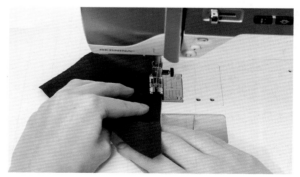

Adjust, holding the pieces as needed.

You may want to pause a couple of times and sew at a slower speed than normal.

The tail end of the fabric gets tricky to hold. When you are about an inch away from the end, gently guide the pieces through the feed dogs.

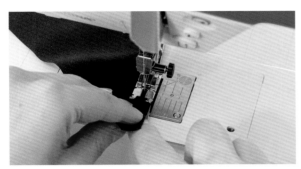
Slow down at the end.

 TIP

A little shift at the tail end of the block does not matter because the blocks are trimmed after they are pieced. Most of the imperfection gets either pressed or quilted down.

10. Sew both of the blocks. Press the seams open. The blocks will distort at this point. If you are making half-square triangles, this is when you trim them to the desired final size.

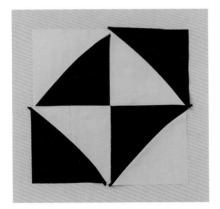
Half-square triangles

 TIP

Press the seams open to avoid bulk in the center. If you are going for an old and imperfect look, press the seams to one side.

HOW TO MAKE HOURGLASS BLOCKS

1. With right sides up, place the blocks on the mat with opposite colors facing. Match the unsewn corners of the blocks.

Restack with opposite colors facing.

2. Cut a gentle freehand curve (no ruler) across the stitched line.

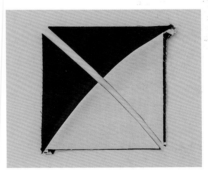
Reslice.

3. Slide the top layer of the right stack to the bottom of that stack.

Slide the top layer to the bottom.

4. Sew the blocks together in the order they appear (follow How to Sew Free-Form Blocks, Steps 7–10, page 14).

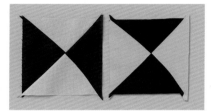

Untrimmed Hourglass blocks

5. You now have 4 Hourglass blocks. Press the seams open to avoid bulk. It helps to have flatter blocks while trimming the squares.

 TIP

Use steam only before trimming the blocks. After trimming, use a dry iron to avoid distortion.

6. Trim to the desired size.

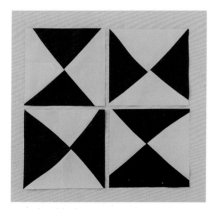

Hourglass blocks

 TIP

Due to the nature of freehand cutting and organic piecing, some blocks may end up smaller than the size suggested in the project. Improvise by adding strips to make up the size. This doesn't detract from the block; it adds character to the quilt.

 TIP

After trimming the blocks, arrange them on a design wall. Free-form blocks can be set in many different ways. Try a few of the examples in the Possibilities section at the end of each project. Combine the layouts or use the blocks for borders.

HOW TO MAKE FLYING GEESE

Starting with an Hourglass block, cut once horizontally to make 2 Flying Geese blocks.

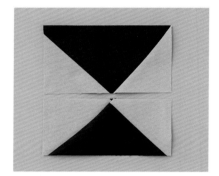

Horizontally slice blocks.

Each stack of 2 squares will make 4 different Flying Geese blocks.

Flying Geese

FABRIC SELECTION

USE WHAT YOU LIKE

My process of fabric selection is simple. I choose fabric combinations that please my eyes. Every quilt becomes an experiment of colors, textures, and shapes. When I start, I am often not sure about the size of the blocks, let alone the quilt.

BORROW FROM THE NEIGHBORS

Use two or three shades of the same color to create depth.

When I worked in a quilt shop, I ended up collecting a huge stash—and I mean *huge* stash—which has turned out to be a blessing. I rely heavily on my stash, but I often run out of the fabric I am working with. I consider that to be a good challenge because it forces me to make do.

So what does *borrow from the neighbors* mean?

I consider the color wheel a neighborhood of colors and shades living happily with one another.

When you run out of one fabric you are working with, bring the next color on the wheel into your quilt. Orange will easily blend with red, and blue with green. This makes your color palette rich and gives more depth to the quilt.

Try to do the same for the value. A pink can easily work in a red quilt. If you use ten reds of the same shade, the quilt becomes boring. Adding pinks, oranges, and even maroon can be complementary to the mix.

I shop with this theory in mind. The biggest advantage: I never run out of fabric in the middle of the project. It also helps to free the creative process. The less your mind worries about using that perfectly matching fabric, the more positive and creative energy can flow into actually making the quilt itself.

WHEN YOU CHOOSE

Contrast Creates Movement

Use contrast in patterns and colors of fabrics to emphasize movement in the patchwork.

While making the quilts for this book, my focus was on showing off curves and imperfections of organic piecing.

Mix Solids, Prints, and Textures

You want to create textural contrast by combining floral prints with plaids, stripes, and dots. However, visually busy quilts can be unpleasant to look at up close. Try adding some solids.

Solid colors can create graphic patterns that make a quilt look bold. They can also provide a way for other textures combined in a quilt—like floral and geometric prints—to shine. Solids also give your eyes a resting space.

EXPERIMENT!

These blocks are fast to make. Make many. You can always use the leftover blocks for the back of the quilt. Let unexpected results work in your favor.

After making just a few stacks of blocks, you will see which fabrics to focus on.

ADD GRAY

Mix gray tones with bright and bold colors to create the sunshine-and-shadow effect.

This is my favorite self-made rule. I love how bright colors shine against the gray. I tend to use gray tones in every quilt.

USE VARIED PRINT SCALES

The scale of the prints used in a block should be relative to the block size.

Large blocks show off large-scale prints. Smaller blocks show up better when solid and smaller-print fabrics are used.

The more solids in a quilt, the more contemporary and graphically bold the quilt will be.

Most important, there is no right or wrong way with this process. If you go with what pleases your eyes, the outcome will reflect your personality.

HOW MUCH FABRIC TO BUY

I buy ⅓ to ½ yard of most fabrics. As a rule, buy many shades of one color instead of a lot of yardage of the same fabric.

Remember: Running out of fabric is an excellent opportunity to be creative and brainstorm about design.

In a nutshell:

- **Be curious** ... thinking of the possibilities.

- **Be bold** ... with selection of patterns, colors, and scale.

- **Be spontaneous** ... with possibilities of setting blocks.

- **Be creative** ... with mixing blocks.

- **Be intuitive** ... listening to your inner voice, making it your own way.

TOOLS NEEDED

- Rotary cutter
- Rotary cutting mat
- Rotating rotary-cutting mat
- Acrylic rulers—squares and rectangles
- Scissors

CRAZY QUILT

FINISHED QUILT: 48½″ × 64½″
FINISHED BLOCK: 8″ × 8″

Pieced by Sujata Shah; machine quilted by Barbara Jackson, Redmond, Washington, 2013

Crazy appliqué wall quilt from India, made with antique lace, cotton, synthetic and wool materials, embroidered yokes, and borders of traditional, regional Indian women's clothing. Gift from Terry Kramzar.

Two things that define crazy quilts are the concept of making do and the visual interest resulting from using odd and irregular bits and pieces of fabrics. Traditionally, crazy blocks are made with scraps stitched to a foundation. The style and materials used in the quilt vary by the countries of origin and the availability of textiles. The crazy quilt is a universal style for quilters needing to make a quilt out of next to nothing.

YARDAGE REQUIREMENTS

Blocks:

- ⅓ yard each of 16 assorted colors of solids

Backing and binding:

- 4⅛ yards

Batting:

- Twin size or a piece 56″ × 72″

CUTTING INSTRUCTIONS

Blocks:

- From each of the 16 fabrics, cut 1 strip 10″ × WOF*. Crosscut 4 squares 10″ × 10″.

Backing:

- Cut 2 pieces 72″ × WOF.

Binding:

- From each piece of backing, cut 2 strips 2½″ × 72″.

WOF = width of fabric

MAKING THE BLOCKS

You will have 16 extra blocks at the end. This is needed to achieve enough variety for the quilt.

1. With right sides up, stack 4 squares 10″ × 10″ of different value and color. Make 16 stacks.

2. Place a stack on the cutting mat, aligning the edges and corners of the squares. Slice through the entire stack on a slant.

Slice.

3. Slide the top right piece to the bottom of the right stack. The squares are now in sewing order.

Slide.

4. Sew together the left and right sides of each square. Press seams open.

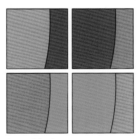

Sewn blocks

5. Repeat Steps 2–4 with the remaining stacks. Change the placement and angle of each cut.

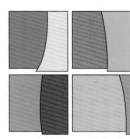

Examples of possibilities for various cuts

6. Regroup 3 or more pieced blocks, each from different stacks. Restack the blocks right side up with the seam of the pieced patches running the same direction on all blocks. Make as many stacks as desired.

7. Repeat Steps 2–5 to make crazy blocks from each stack.

Stack, then slice.   Slide, then sew.

8. Trim the blocks to 8½″ × 8½″.

Trim.

> **TIP**
>
> **For smaller patches:** Start with a larger square to make a block with smaller crazy patches. Just remember: More cuts mean more seams, so the final block will be smaller.

> **TIP**
>
> **Trim last:** Finish making and then measure all the blocks before trimming them. I try to get maximum inches out of my blocks. Trim to the size of the smallest block or add strips if a few are small.

ASSEMBLY

1. Arrange blocks on the design wall in 8 horizontal rows, each containing 6 blocks.

2. Shuffle the blocks around.

3. When you are satisfied with the layout, sew the blocks into rows. Press the block seams in alternating directions from row to row.

4. Sew the rows together. Press all the row seams in the same direction.

TIP

Optional border: You will have 16 extra blocks to play with. Use them on the back or make an optional border. For a border, cut the extra blocks into strips of the desired width and sew them together lengthwise.

FINISHING

1. Sew 2 backing pieces together lengthwise. *Note:* If you added a border, be sure the backing is large enough.

2. Layer and baste together the backing, batting, and top.

3. Machine or hand quilt.

4. Sew the binding strips together with diagonal seams. Bind the quilt. *Note:* If you added an optional border, check that you have enough binding length to go around your quilt. Add an extra binding strip if needed.

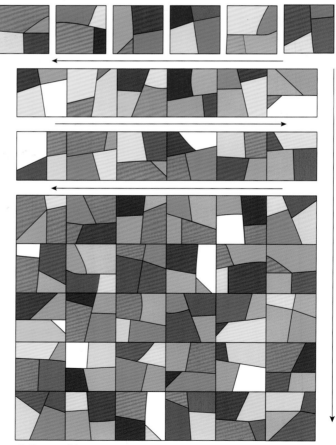

Quilt assembly

POSSIBILITIES

- Set the blocks on point.

- Add setting squares between the blocks.

- Add setting triangles around the edges.

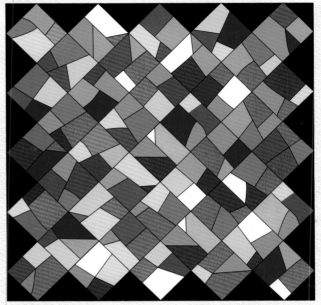

Mostly crazy

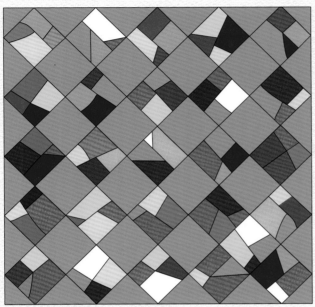

Somewhat crazy

Allover crazy

RAIL FENCE

FINISHED QUILT: 80½″ × 96½″
FINISHED BLOCK: 16″ × 16″

Pieced by Sujata Shah; machine quilted by Barbara Jackson, Redmond, Washington, 2013

Photo by Sujata Shah

Hand-woven straw basket

Photos by Sujata Shah

Basket closeup

Kuba cloth from Kenya

YARDAGE REQUIREMENTS

Blocks:

- ⅓ yard each of 15 to 20 light to medium fabrics*
- ⅓ yard each of 15 to 20 medium to dark fabrics*

Backing:

- 7⅝ yards

Binding:

- ⅞ yard

Batting:

- Queen size or a piece 88″ × 104″

* The more fabrics you use, the more variety in the finished quilt.

This basket was a happy discovery at an import store. The cross-weave of the diagonal straw varying in widths creates movement. Hand stripped, uneven straw makes a straight line in this organic texture. Kuba cloth is similar in texture and created with straw and raffia.

CUTTING INSTRUCTIONS

Blocks:
- From each of the block fabrics, cut a strip 5½″ × WOF*; crosscut each strip into 2 strips 5½″ × 20″.

Backing:
- Cut 3 pieces 88″ × WOF.

Binding:
- Cut 10 strips 2½″ × WOF.

* WOF = width of fabric

MAKING THE BLOCKS

1. With right sides up, stack 4 strips: 2 of the same light to medium and 2 of the same medium to dark.

2. Arrange the stack with the values in alternating order. Make 30 stacks.

Stack.

3. Place a stack on the cutting mat, aligning the corners and edges of the strips. Slice the stack lengthwise with a gentle curve from the bottom to the top edge.

Slice.

> **TIP**
>
> Slice about 2″; then hold the left bottom edge with your other hand to prevent the fabric from shifting while cutting. Steam-press the stack just before cutting to temporarily bond the layers.

4. Slide the top right strip of the stack to the bottom of the right stack. The strips are now in the correct sewing order.

Slide.

5. Sew together the strips in the order they appear. Match the points at the top of the strips. *Note: Sewn strips will look out of shape and visibly uneven.*

6. Sew all 4 units. Press seams toward the dark fabric.

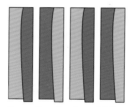

Four pieced strips with inverted colors

> **TIP**
>
> Slight stretching while ironing helps to flatten these units.

7. Place each pieced strip unit individually on the cutting mat. Trim strips to 4½″ wide.

8. Crosscut each trimmed strip into 4 units 4½″ × 4½″.

Crosscut trimmed strips.

9. Arrange the 16 units in a block.

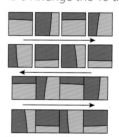

Block assembly

10. Sew the Rail Fence units into 4 rows, each containing 4 units.

11. Press the seams in alternating directions from row to row.

12. Sew together the rows. Press these seams open.

13. Repeat Steps 3–12 to make 30 blocks.

ASSEMBLY

1. Arrange the blocks in 6 horizontal rows, each containing 5 blocks.

2. Sew the blocks into rows. Press the seams in alternating directions from row to row.

3. Sew the rows together. Press the seams in the same direction.

FINISHING

1. Sew the backing pieces together lengthwise.

2. Layer and baste together the backing, batting, and quilt top.

3. Machine or hand quilt.

4. Sew the binding strips together with diagonal seams. Bind the quilt.

Quilt assembly

POSSIBILITIES

- Set the blocks in inventive ways.

- Make 15 Rail Fence blocks and 15 mirror-image Rail Fence blocks to make the Square Steps pattern.

- Rotate the blocks in every row to make the Zigzag Steps pattern.

- Sew Rail Fence units into a variation on the Whirligig block.

- Combine the units (made with ethnic or contemporary fabrics) to replicate mud cloth and waxed batiks from Africa.

Square Steps

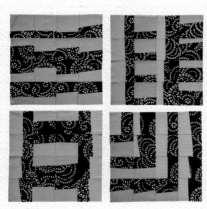

A variation on the Whirligig block

Mud cloth variations

Zigzag Steps

Hopscotch, 88½″ × 88½″, by LeeAnn Decker, Seattle, Washington, 2011

Whirligig blocks and Chinese Coins border

TORAN

FINISHED QUILT: 56½″ × 56½″
FINISHED BLOCK: 8″ × 8″

Machine pieced and hand quilted by Sujata Shah, Chester Springs, Pennsylvania, 2011

Toran hanging over a pathway leading from the front gate to the entrance of a fort in Rajasthan, India

Photo by Sujata Shah

In India, string banners, known as **torans**, are used during cultural celebrations to create arches in doorways and pathways to welcome guests. Torans made from fresh leaves and marigolds strung on cotton strings adorn the doorways of private homes on a daily basis.

In spite of all cotton materials and perfectly squared-up blocks in this quilt, gently curved piecing and organic hand quilting create the illusion of a toran in a soft, cool breeze.

YARDAGE REQUIREMENTS

Blocks and borders:

- ¾ yard each of 8 medium to dark green, khaki, and brown solids
- 2½–3 yards total of varying-width strips 1″ to 2″ wide × at least 10″ long of bright-colored solids and prints

Backing:

- 3⅝ yards

Binding:

- ⅝ yard

Batting:

- Twin size or a piece 64″ × 64″

CUTTING INSTRUCTIONS

Green, khaki, and brown solids:
From each ¾ yard:

- Cut 1 strip 10″ × WOF*. Crosscut to make 18–22 squares 10″ × 10″ for the blocks.

- Cut 5–7 varying-width strips 1″–2″ × WOF. Crosscut into 10″ sections for the borders.

Bright-colored solids and prints:

- Cut all strips into 10″ sections.

Backing:

- Cut 2 pieces each 64″ × WOF.

Binding:

- Cut 7 strips 2½″ × WOF.

WOF = width of fabric

TIP

Always make a few extra blocks. It will give you flexibility in the final layout and design. Use leftover blocks in the backing or in another quilt.

MAKING THE BLOCKS

1. Sew together strips of bright-colored solids and prints to make 18–22 string squares 10″ × 10″. Press seams to one side.

String squares.

2. With right sides up, stack 4 squares 10″ × 10″: 2 different string squares and 2 different solid squares.

3. Arrange the stack with the squares in alternating order. Make at least 9 stacks.

Stack.

4. Place a stack on the cutting mat, aligning the edges and corners. Slice a gentle curve through all 4 layers.

Slice.

5. Slide a half triangle from the top to the bottom of the right stack.

Slide.

6. Sew together the half-square triangles in the order they appear in the stack. Press seams to the solid halves.

Sewn blocks.

Each string block will produce a concave and convex half-square triangle matched with a different solid.

Concave and convex half-square triangles.

7. Repeat Steps 4–6 to make at least 36 blocks.

8. Trim the blocks to 8½″ × 8½″.

Trim.

STRING BORDERS

1. From the border strips, make string squares measuring 10″ × 10″. Press the seams in one direction.

2. Cut 2 strips from each block measuring 4½″ × 9½″.

Cut string block.

3. Sew the strips from different blocks to make 2 side borders 48½″ × 4½″ and top and bottom borders, each measuring 56½″ × 4½″. Set them aside.

Border construction

ASSEMBLY

1. Sew the blocks into rows. Press in alternating directions from row to row.

2. Sew the rows together. Press the seams in one direction.

3. Sew borders onto the sides. Press the seams toward the borders.

4. Add the top and bottom borders. Press the seams toward the borders.

FINISHING

1. Sew the backing pieces together lengthwise.

2. Layer and baste together the backing, batting, and quilt top.

3. Machine or hand quilt.

4. Sew the binding strips together with diagonal seams. Bind the quilt.

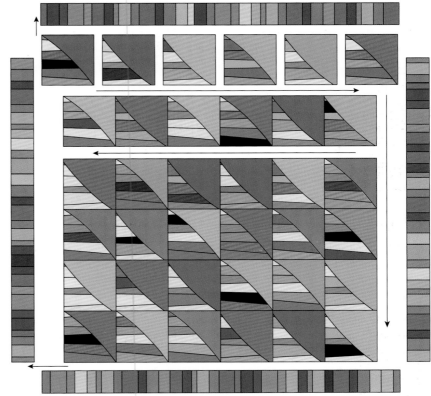

Quilt assembly

■ Set the blocks in a different arrangement. String blocks are fun to play with.

■ Make a diamond block: Sew 4 half-square triangles with the strings to the center, forming a diamond square. The busyness of the string-pieced triangles creates sparkle against solid backgrounds.

■ Randomly arrange string-pieced triangles to make a free-form zigzag, which will create chaotic movement and texture in a contained form.

■ This is a perfect pattern to show off large-scale prints. Use them to create movement in the background.

■ Follow the instructions from *Crazy Quilt* (page 19) to make crazy blocks for the background. Use crazy quilt blocks with string blocks to make a quilt reminiscent of streamers.

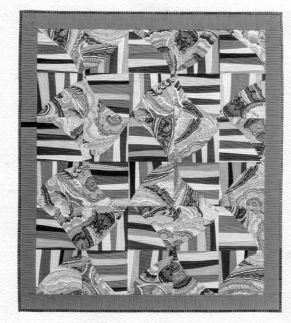

Guadalajara Salsa, 45½″ × 53¼″, pieced and machine quilted by Dorothy (Sally) LeBoeuf, Edmonds, Washington, 2013

Diamond

Free-form zigzag

Summer Breeze, 56½″ × 63½″, pieced and machine quilted by Sujata Shah, Chester Springs, Pennsylvania, 2012

HOURGLASS
BABY QUILT

FINISHED QUILT: 42½″ × 43½″
FINISHED BLOCKS: 6″ × 6″ and 6″ × 8″

Machine pieced and hand quilted by Sujata Shah, Chester Springs, Pennsylvania, 2013

Ralli quilt from Pakistan, hand pieced and hand quilted, maker unknown. Gift from a friend, Sufia Shahid Haq, Islamabad, Pakistan; collection of Sujata Shah.

YARDAGE REQUIREMENTS

Blocks and borders:

- ¾ yard dark green
- ⅝ yard medium green
- ⅜ yard light green
- ¾ yard dark red
- ⅜ yard medium red
- ¾ yard light red

Backing:

- 3 yards

Binding:

- ½ yard red

Batting:

- Twin size or a piece 50″ × 51″

Modern quilting tools have not influenced the age-old craft of ralli quiltmaking. For the most part, artisans in rural areas of India and Pakistan make quilts by hand with very few tools.

The use of scissors and handwork is quite evident in the sashing. Forced piecing of the blue star with puckered corners and not-so-round circles in the center adds whimsy and soul to this ralli quilt.

Variation in scale, missing corners, and two different shades of blue in the triangle border illustrate the concept of making do as a way of life around the world.

CUTTING INSTRUCTIONS

Dark green:
- Cut 3 strips 8″ × WOF*; crosscut 13 squares 8″ × 8″ for the quilt center blocks.

Medium green:
- Cut 1 strip 8″ × WOF; crosscut 4 squares 8″ × 8″ for the side borders.
- Cut 1 strip 10″ × WOF; crosscut 4 rectangles 8″ × 10″ for the cornerstones.

* WOF = width of fabric

Light green:
- Cut 1 strip 10″ × WOF; crosscut 5 rectangles 8″ × 10″ for the top and bottom borders.

Dark red:
- Cut 3 strips 8″ × WOF; crosscut 13 squares 8″ × 8″ for the quilt center blocks.

Medium red:
- Cut 1 strip 10″ × WOF; crosscut 5 rectangles 8″ × 10″ for the top and bottom borders.

Light red:
- Cut 1 strip 8″ × WOF; crosscut 4 squares 8″ × 8″ for the side borders.
- Cut 1 strip 10″ × WOF; crosscut 4 rectangles 8″ × 10″ for the cornerstones.
- Cut 2 strips 2″ × 42½″ for the skinny top and bottom borders.

Backing:
- Cut 2 pieces 50″ × WOF.

Binding:
- Cut 6 strips 2½″ × WOF.

MAKING THE BLOCKS

1. With right sides up, stack 2 squares 8″ × 8″: 1 dark green and 1 dark red. Make 13 stacks.

Stack.

2. Place a stack on the cutting mat, aligning the edges and corners of the squares. Slice diagonally once through all layers from bottom right to top left corner.

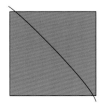

Slice.

3. Slide the top right triangle to the bottom of the right stack.

Slide.

4. Sew together the triangles in the order they now appear in the stack. Press the seams open to avoid bulk in the center.

Sew.

> **TIP**
>
> Always match the starting points of the triangles. When sewn, the square will have a tail. This is quite normal.

5. With right sides up, restack the squares in an alternating order with red and green triangles on opposite sides of each layer.

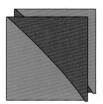

Restack.

While reslicing the blocks, slice slightly away from the center of the block to make floating triangles.

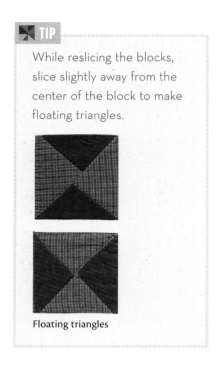

Floating triangles

6. Roughly align the unsewn corners of the squares. With a slight curve, diagonally reslice the stack.

Reslice.

7. Slide the right half of the block to the bottom of the right stack.

Slide.

8. Sew the halves together to make Hourglass blocks.

9. Trim the blocks to 6½″ × 6½″. You now have 2 blocks with inverted colors.

Trim.

Trim blocks one at a time and off-centered for more variation and interest. Position the square ruler in one corner.

10. Repeat Steps 2–9 to make blocks from the remaining stacks of squares. This will make 6 extra blocks.

Top and Bottom Border Blocks

1. With right sides up, stack 2 rectangles 8″ × 10″: 1 medium red and 1 light green. Make 5 stacks.

2. Follow Making the Blocks, Steps 2–10 (page 37), to make 10 Hourglass blocks. Trim the blocks to 6½″ × 8½″.

Blocks for top and bottom borders

Side Border Blocks

1. With right sides up, stack 2 squares 8″ × 8″: 1 medium green and 1 light red. Make 4 stacks.

2. Follow Making the Blocks, Steps 2–10 (page 37), to make 8 Hourglass blocks. Trim the blocks to 6½″ × 6½″.

Cornerstones

1. With right sides up, stack 2 rectangles 8″ × 10″: 1 medium green and 1 light red. Make 4 stacks.

2. Follow Making the Blocks, Steps 2–10 (page 37), to make 8 Hourglass blocks. Trim the blocks to 6½″ × 8½″. (You will only use 4 of these blocks.)

Rectangle blocks for cornerstones

ASSEMBLY

1. Follow the quilt assembly diagram to arrange the blocks for the center and borders.

2. Sew the blocks in rows. Press the seams in alternating directions from row to row.

3. Attach the skinny borders to the top and bottom. Press the seams toward the borders.

FINISHING

1. Sew the backing pieces together lengthwise.

2. Layer and baste together the backing, batting, and quilt top.

3. Machine or hand quilt.

4. Sew the binding strips together with diagonal seams. Bind the quilt.

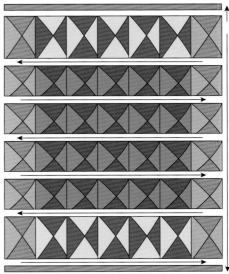

Quilt assembly

 POSSIBILITIES

- Experiment with color, size, and setting of the blocks.

- Group stacks of 4 different blocks, each stack containing a set of contrasting blocks. Make it your own!

Summer Blues

Blue Diamonds, 20½" × 20½", machine pieced by Sujata Shah, Chester Springs, Pennsylvania, 2012

HOURGLASS TWIST

FINISHED QUILT: 62½˝ × 62½˝
FINISHED BLOCK: 8˝ × 8˝

Machine pieced by Sujata Shah; machine quilted by Barbara Jackson, Redmond, Washington, 2013

THE ROOT CONNECTION

Ralli quilt, Rajasthan, India

Kinari—a Hindi word; used for borders on textiles such as heavily decorated trims or edges of the sleeves and hems of traditional clothing and saris. Also, a widely used motif by Indian quiltmakers, depicting the mountains at the edge of the deserts.

Quarter-square triangles not only make the hourglass border but also give the appearance of two prairie point borders.

YARDAGE REQUIREMENTS

Blocks:

Use 2 or 3 shades of the same color to create depth in the palette.

- ½ yard each of 12 medium to dark pink and red prints and solids
- ½ yard each of 12 yellow and lime green tone-on-tone prints

Borders:

- ⅝ yard dark pink solid
- 1¼ yards dark green solid

Backing:

- 4⅛ yards

Binding:

- ⅝ yard

Batting:

- Twin size or a piece 70″ × 70″

CUTTING INSTRUCTIONS

Extra yellow/lime green and red/pink squares are cut to allow for variety in the quilt.

Pink/red:
- From each fabric, cut 2 strips 6″ × WOF*. Crosscut 9 squares 6″ × 6″ for blocks. (You will use 98.)

Yellow/lime green:
- From each fabric, cut 2 strips 6″ × WOF. Crosscut 9 squares 6″ × 6″ for blocks.

Dark pink solid:
- Cut 5 strips 1½″ × WOF for the inner border.

Dark green solid:
- Cut 13 strips 1½″ × WOF for inner and outer borders.
- Cut 3 strips 6″ × WOF. Crosscut 18 squares 6″ × 6″ for the blocks. (You will use 15.)

Backing:
- Cut 2 pieces 70″ × WOF.

Binding:
- Cut 7 strips 2½″ × WOF.

* WOF = width of fabric

MAKING THE BLOCKS

1. With right sides up, stack 4 squares 6″ × 6″: 2 of the same pink/red and 2 of the same yellow/lime green.

2. Arrange the stack with the colors in alternating order. Make 36 stacks.

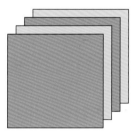

Stack.

3. Follow *Hourglass Baby Quilt*, Making the Blocks, Steps 2–8 (page 37), to make 144 Hourglass blocks.

4. Trim the blocks to 4½″ × 4½″. From each stack you will get 4 Hourglass blocks: 2 each of inverted colors.

5. Arrange 4 Hourglass blocks into an Hourglass Twist block.

6. Follow the block assembly diagram to make 36 Hourglass Twist blocks. Press the seams in alternating directions from row to row.

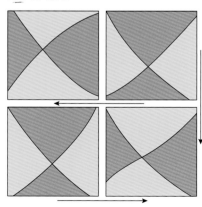

Hourglass Twist block assembly

Blocks for Borders

1. With right sides up, stack 4 squares 6″ × 6″: 2 different pink/red, 1 yellow/lime green, and 1 dark green.

2. Arrange the stack with yellow/lime green on the top, followed by pink/red, dark green, and pink/red. Make 13 stacks.

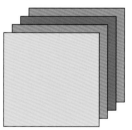

Stack for the borders

3. Follow *Hourglass Baby Quilt*, Making the Blocks, Steps 2–4 (page 37), to make 52 half-square triangles.

4. Restack the half-square triangles in an alternating order, with pink/red on the opposite side of each layer. *Note:* While restacking the half-square triangles to make Hourglass blocks, keep in mind that the second yellow/lime green square was replaced by a dark green square.

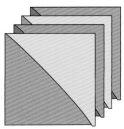

Restack.

5. Follow *Hourglass Baby Quilt*, Making the Blocks, Steps 6–8 (page 38), to make 52 Hourglass blocks.

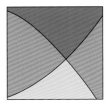

Block for the border.

6. Trim blocks to 4½˝ × 4½˝.

Borders

INNER DARK PINK BORDER

1. Sew the 5 dark pink fabric strips 1½˝ × WOF end to end.

2. Cut 2 strips 1½˝ × 48½˝ and 2 strips 1½˝ × 50½˝.

INNER DARK GREEN BORDER

1. Sew 6 inner dark green border strips 1½˝ × WOF end to end.

2. Cut 2 strips 1½˝ × 50½˝ and 2 strips 1½˝ × 52½˝.

CORNERSTONE BLOCKS

1. With right sides up, stack 4 squares 6˝ × 6˝: 2 different yellow/lime green and 2 dark green.

2. Arrange the stack with the colors in alternating order.

3. Follow *Hourglass Baby Quilt*, Making the Blocks, Steps 2–4 (page 37), to make 4 half-square triangles.

4. Trim blocks to 4½˝ × 4½˝.

PIECED OUTER BORDER

1. Sew 4 borders 4½˝ × 52½˝ each with 13 Hourglass blocks.

2. Sew cornerstones at both ends of 2 of the borders to make the top and bottom borders.

Pieced side border

Pieced top and bottom border

OUTER DARK GREEN BORDER

1. Sew the remaining 7 dark green outer border strips 1½˝ × WOF end to end.

2. Cut 2 dark green side outer borders 1½˝ × 60½˝ and 2 top and bottom outer borders 1½˝ × 62½˝.

ASSEMBLY

1. Following the quilt assembly diagram, arrange the blocks in 6 rows, with each row containing 6 blocks.

2. Sew the blocks into rows. Press the seams in alternating directions from row to row.

3. Sew the rows together. Press the seams in one direction.

4. Sew the dark pink inner borders 1½˝ × 48½˝ to the sides of the quilt. Then sew the dark pink inner borders 1½˝ × 50½˝ to the top and bottom of the quilt. Press the seams toward the borders.

5. Sew the dark green inner borders 1½˝ × 50½˝ to the sides of the quilt. Then sew the dark green inner borders 1½˝ × 52½˝ to the top and bottom of the quilt. Press the seams toward the dark green borders.

6. Sew the pieced borders to the sides of the quilt. Then sew the pieced borders with the cornerstones to the top and bottom of the quilt. Press the seams toward the pieced borders.

7. Sew the dark green outer borders 1½˝ × 60½˝ to the sides of the quilt. Then sew the dark green outer borders 1½˝ × 62½˝ to the top and bottom of the quilt. Press the seams toward the dark green borders.

Quilt assembly

FINISHING

1. Sew the backing pieces together lengthwise.

2. Layer and baste together the backing, batting, and quilt top.

3. Machine or hand quilt.

4. Sew the binding strips together with diagonal seams. Bind the quilt.

POSSIBILITIES

- Use 2 different light and dark fabrics.

- Group a light and a dark square and make an Hourglass block. Slice it horizontally to make Flying Geese blocks. The width of the block will be the same but the height of the geese will change.

Tipsy Triangle border

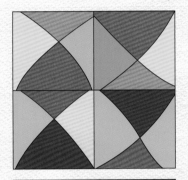

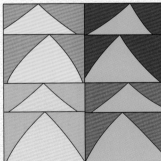

Flying North

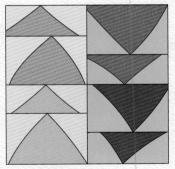

Tipsy Triangles

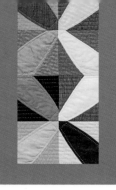

WINDMILLS

FINISHED QUILT: 48½″ × 48½″
FINISHED BLOCK: 6″ × 6″

Pieced and hand quilted by Sujata Shah, Chester Springs, Pennsylvania, 2013

Photo by Vilas Malankar

Windmill on a farm in New Holland, Pennsylvania

Hand quilting by Sujata Shah

YARDAGE REQUIREMENTS

Blocks:
- ¼ yard each of 16 assorted solids (4 total yards of fabric)

Backing:
- 3¼ yards

Binding:
- ½ yard

Batting:
- Twin size or a piece 56″ × 56″

I was seven when I made my first paper pinwheel with my brother. He taught me how to make paper airplanes, boats, birds, and vases, among many other things. The word **origami** was not in our vocabulary, but we spent hours marking and drawing, cutting and gluing papers from recycled notebooks during long summer days. I loved coloring them, and he enjoyed constructing them to perfection. We used to stand on the balcony, with our hands stuck out, holding pinwheels and watching them spin in the cool summer breeze.

Although inspired by windmills on Amish farms, this quilt connects me to those memories of my childhood. I still make windmills and pinwheels, but now I paint them with thread.

CUTTING INSTRUCTIONS

Assorted solids:
- From each cut 1 strip 8″ × WOF*; crosscut 4 squares 8″ × 8″ for a total of 64 squares for the blocks.

Backing:
- Cut 2 pieces 56″ × WOF.

Binding:
- Cut 6 strips 2½″ × WOF.

* WOF = width of fabric

MAKING THE BLOCKS

1. With right sides up, stack 4 squares 8″ × 8″ of contrasting value.

2. Arrange the stack with the values in alternating order. Make 16 stacks.

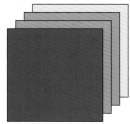

Stack.

3. Place a stack on the cutting mat, aligning the edges and corners of the squares. Slice a leaf-shaped wedge in the center of the stack.

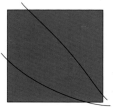

Slice.

> ✳ **TIP**
>
> To cut the wedge with a slight curve, slide the ruler as you cut ever so gently, keeping the rotary cutter along the edge of the ruler.
>
> Use scissors to cut organic shapes. If using scissors, pin the 3 sections of the stack to avoid any shifting of the layers.

4. Slide the top leaf to the bottom of the stack. The blocks are now in sewing order.

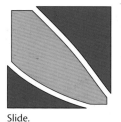

Slide.

5. Starting with the top layer, sew the leaf to the left background piece. Chain piece the remaining leaves.

Sew left background to leaf.

> ✳ **TIP**
>
> To avoid distorting the unsewn edges, do not press until the second side of the background is pieced.

6. Sew the right side of the background to the left half of the block. Press the seams to the center. The blocks will look like kites. This is perfectly normal.

Sew right background to leaf.

7. Trim the blocks to 6½″ × 6½″.

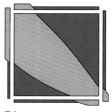

Trim.

8. Repeat Steps 3–7 for the remaining 15 stacks.

ASSEMBLY

1. Arrange the blocks in 8 rows, with 8 blocks per row.

2. Sew the blocks together in horizontal rows. Press the seams in alternating directions from row to row.

3. Sew the rows together. Press the seams in one direction.

FINISHING

1. Sew the backing pieces together lengthwise.

2. Layer and baste together the backing, batting, and quilt top.

3. Machine or hand quilt.

4. Sew the binding strips together with diagonal seams. Bind the quilt.

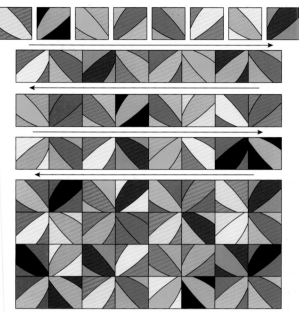

Quilt assembly

 # POSSIBILITIES

- Choose 2 colors and make a block similar to a Robbing Peter to Pay Paul block.

- Stack an even number of squares of each color to make blocks alternating in positive and negative space.

- Make larger blocks.

- Stack 4 squares, 2 each of 2 different colors.

- Arrange the blocks radiating outward.

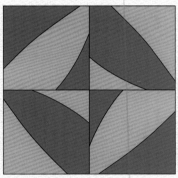

Robbing Peter to Pay Paul

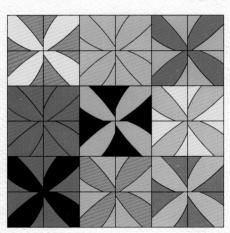

Happy Days

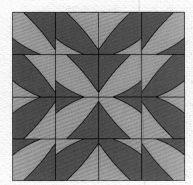

Fish in the Pond

ROCKY ROAD TO KANSAS

FINISHED QUILT: 48½″ × 48½″
FINISHED BLOCK: 8″ × 8″

Pieced and machine quilted by Sujata Shah, Chester Springs, Pennsylvania, 2012

Detail of appliqué ralli quilt from western India, maker unknown

YARDAGE REQUIREMENTS

Blocks:

- ½ yard each of 12 different prints

Backing:

- 3¼ yards

Binding:

- ½ yard

Batting:

- Twin size or a piece 56″ × 56″

Patterns and design are a constantly evolving process. Every step in the process leads to a new discovery. This block was inspired by the leaf-shaped blocks in *Windmills* (page 46). In many ways, it resembles a commonly used shape in a reverse-appliquéd ralli quilt.

CUTTING INSTRUCTIONS

Blocks:
- From each of the prints, cut 2 strips 6″ × WOF*. Subcut into 12 squares 6″ × 6″.

Backing:
- Cut 2 pieces 56″ × WOF.

Binding:
- Cut 6 strips 2½″ × WOF.

* WOF = width of fabric

MAKING THE BLOCKS

1. With right sides up, stack 4 squares 6″ × 6″ of 4 different fabrics. Make 4 identical stacks, with squares in the same order. This is very important.

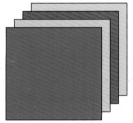

Stack.

> ✖ **TIP**
>
> Use pins to hold grouped stacks together until you are ready to use them.

2. Place a stack on the cutting mat, aligning the edges and corners of the squares. Diagonally slice a leaf shape through all 4 layers of all 4 stacks.

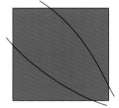

Slice.

> ✖ **TIP**
>
> Make sure the points of the leaves are just 1″ wide. It helps to have thinner points at the tip (they end up a little wide after trimming).

3. Follow *Windmills*, Making the Blocks, Steps 4–6 (page 48).

4. Trim the Windmill units to 4½″ × 4½″. Repeat Steps 2 and 3 for the remaining 3 identical stacks.

5. Combine 1 Windmill unit from each identical stack to make Rocky Road to Kansas blocks.

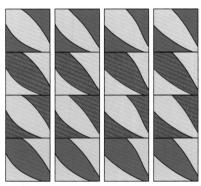

Sets of Windmill units

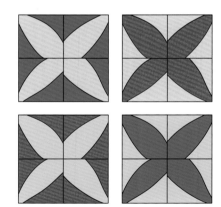

Rocky Road to Kansas blocks

6. Sew together 4 Windmill units to make a Rocky Road to Kansas block. Press the seams open. Make 4.

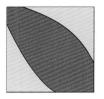

Rocky Road to Kansas block construction

7. Repeat Steps 1–6 a total of 8 more times to make 36 Rocky Road to Kansas blocks.

ASSEMBLY

1. Arrange the blocks in 6 rows, with 6 blocks per row.

2. Sew together the blocks in horizontal rows. Press the seams in alternating directions from row to row.

 TIP

Avoid stretching the fabric while pressing. Do not overpress.

3. Sew the rows together. Press the seams in one direction.

FINISHING

1. Sew the backing pieces together lengthwise.

2. Layer and baste together the backing, batting, and quilt top.

3. Machine or hand quilt.

4. Sew the binding strips together with diagonal seams. Bind the quilt.

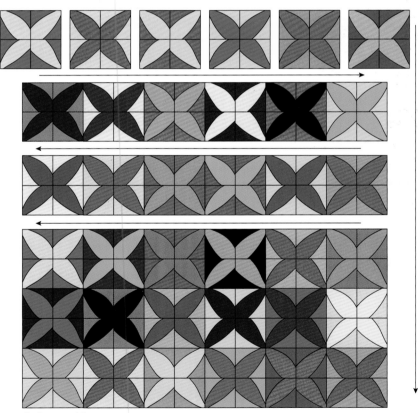

Quilt assembly

- Be curious. Arrange the blocks in different ways.

- Make an equal number of Windmill and Rocky Road to Kansas blocks. Arrange them horizontally, alternating the order.

- Trim the blocks by centering a square ruler on each one to get somewhat identical finished blocks.

Rocky Road to Kansas and Windmill blocks paired

Wax-resist batik from Africa

Windmill block (at left) and Rocky Road to Kansas block

LATTICE

FINISHED QUILT: 60½″ × 60½″
FINISHED BLOCK: 6″ × 6″

Pieced, hand quilted, and hand tied by Sujata Shah, Chester Springs, Pennsylvania, 2013

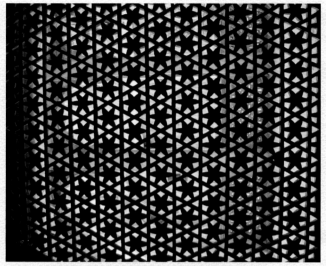

Photos by Sujata Shah

Carved-wood window at a fort in Rajasthan, India

Lattice was inspired by hand-carved windows of an ancient fort. Carved windows not only were an architectural feature but also acted as shelter from harsh elements of desert sandstorms and intense heat, while allowing cooler air in at night. The stars in the hexagons appear uniform but have irregularities in their size and thickness. The shades and tones of structures beyond are as graphic as the window itself.

YARDAGE REQUIREMENTS

Blocks:

- ⅞ yard blue
- ⅞ yard each of 2 black prints
- ⅞ yard each of 2 deep red prints
- ⅞ yard each of 2 salmon pink prints
- ⅞ yard each of 3 medium to dark tan prints

Backing:

- 4 yards

Binding:

- ⅝ yard

Batting:

- Twin piece or a piece 68″ × 68″

CUTTING INSTRUCTIONS

Blocks:

- From each block fabric, cut 3 strips 9″ × WOF*. Crosscut 10 squares 9″ × 9″.

Backing:

- Cut 2 pieces 68″ × WOF.

Binding:

- Cut 7 strips 2½″ × WOF.

WOF = width of fabric

MAKING THE BLOCKS

1. With right sides up, stack 4 contrasting squares 9″ × 9″. Make 25 stacks.

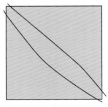

Stack.

2. Place a stack on the cutting mat, aligning the edges and corners of the squares. Slice a diagonal wedge in the center of the stack.

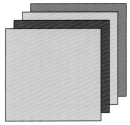

Slice.

> **✂ TIP**
>
> The 2 ends of the lattice wedge should be a little narrower than the center. Aim for 1½″ width on the ends and 2″ in the center. The center wedge is the lattice and the triangle sides are the background.

3. Slide the top lattice piece to the bottom of the stack. The blocks are now in sewing order.

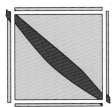

Slide.

4. Starting with the top layer, sew the lattice to the left background piece. Chain piece the remaining lattices.

Sew left background to lattice.

> **✂ TIP**
>
> To avoid distorting the unsewn edges, do not press until the second side of the background is pieced.

5. Sew the right side of the background to the left half of the block in the same order. Press the seams away from the center. The block will look like a kite after all 3 pieces are sewn together.

Sew right background to lattice.

6. Repeat Steps 2–5 with the remaining stacks to make 100 blocks.

7. Trim the blocks to 6½″ × 6½″.

Trim.

ASSEMBLY

1. Arrange the blocks in 10 horizontal rows, each containing 10 blocks.

2. Sew the blocks into rows. Press the seams in alternating directions from row to row.

3. Sew the rows together. Press the seams in one direction.

FINISHING

1. Sew the backing pieces together lengthwise.

2. Layer and baste together the backing, batting, and quilt top.

3. Machine or hand quilt.

4. Sew the binding strips together with diagonal seams. Bind the quilt.

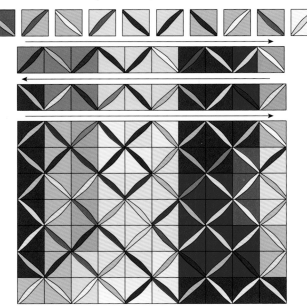

Quilt assembly

 POSSIBILITIES

- Mix up the blocks. With free-form blocks, each fabric repeats in another block. No matter how you choose to arrange them, there is a balance of color and pattern throughout the quilt.

- Try different settings, such as zigzag or diamond.

- Use the blocks in borders.

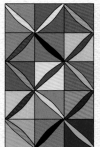

Border options

Streamers, 24½″ × 32½″, pieced and machine quilted by Kelly Meanix, Downingtown, Pennsylvania, 2013

Gift to Sujata Shah

CROSSROADS

FINISHED QUILT: 60½″ × 60½″
FINISHED BLOCK: 6″ × 6″

Pieced by Sujata Shah, Chester Springs, Pennsylvania; machine quilted by Barbara Jackson, Redmond, Washington, 2004

Waxed batik print, resist-dyed cloth

YARDAGE REQUIREMENTS

Blocks:

- ⅓ yard each of 25 prints and solids (8⅓ yards total)

Backing:

- 4 yards

Binding:

- ⅝ yard

Batting:

- Twin size or a piece 68″ × 68″

Teaching workshops inspired by the quilts of Gee's Bend was a process of self-discovery. Although I personally never experienced a harsh life, their stories reminded me of many in India who had. Trying to get in the mind-set of those women, I presented the class with various challenges for "making do." Some students tried every challenge with an open heart; others had difficulty relating to it. Staying away from abundant fabric choices and unlearning the rules of quilting was difficult. Students needing to find perfection, even in the idea of celebrating imperfection, kept undoing seams and restitching patches until they were happy. Others cut and sewed every wonky seam in anticipation of what was unfolding.

I sensed a shift in me—standing at the crossroads of being perfect and being free as a quilter.

CUTTING INSTRUCTIONS

Blocks:
- From each fabric, cut 1 strip 9″ × WOF*; crosscut into 4 squares 9″ × 9″.

Backing:
- Cut 2 pieces 68″ × WOF.

Binding:
- Cut 7 strips 2½″ × WOF.

* WOF = width of fabric

MAKING THE BLOCKS

1. Follow *Lattice*, Making the Blocks, Steps 1–6 (page 57). Use 9″ × 9″ squares for this project. As you finish constructing the Lattice blocks, replace them in their original order in their original stacks. This is very important.

2. Continue with the same stacks of blocks, with right sides up. Be sure that all wedges run in the same direction. Match the unsewn corners of the blocks in the stack.

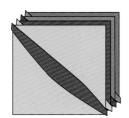

Stack.

3. Crosscut a wedge through all 4 blocks in the opposite direction.

Reslice.

 TIP

Crosscut the wedge about ½″ wider than the pieced wedge to allow for the seam allowance.

4. Slide the top wedge to the bottom of the center stack.

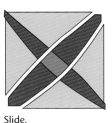

Slide.

5. Follow *Lattice*, Making the Blocks, Steps 4 and 5 (page 57) for all 4 blocks.

6. Repeat Steps 2–5 for each stack to make 100 Crossroads blocks. *Note:* The blocks will look like they have extended corners. The wedges will look a little skinnier after they are stitched. This is perfectly normal.

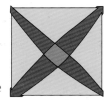

Crossroads block

 **TIP**

Every cut is a freehand cut, so there will be no matching seams and no consistent width of the wedges or points for this block. This is the beauty of the process. Enjoy every wonky line and mismatched point. These enhance the personality of the quilt.

Cross blocks with different widths

7. Trim the blocks to 6½" × 6½".

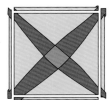

Trim.

✕ TIP

Before trimming, measure the blocks. I like to keep the narrow tips of wedges as much as possible. If I can trim each block to 7" × 7", I prefer that to trimming off perfectly usable parts. It gives me flexibility to make a larger quilt or use fewer blocks.

ASSEMBLY

✕ TIP

Place the blocks on a design wall and use a reducing glass for perspective. Arrange and rearrange the blocks until you are happy.

1. Arrange the blocks in 10 horizontal rows, each containing 10 blocks.

2. Sew the blocks into rows. Press the seams in alternating directions from row to row.

3. Sew the rows together. Press the seams in one direction.

FINISHING

1. Sew the backing pieces together lengthwise.

2. Layer and baste together the backing, batting, and quilt top.

3. Machine or hand quilt.

4. Sew the binding strips together with diagonal seams. Bind the quilt.

Quilt assembly

POSSIBILITIES

Use solids with plaids and stripes. Watch new patterns evolve and recede as fabrics and colors fade into each other.

Sparklers, 72" × 84", machine pieced by Helen Knopf, Redmond, Washington; machine quilted by Barbara Jackson, Redmond, Washington, 2006

New Beginnings, 30½" × 30½", machine pieced and hand quilted by Sujata Shah, Chester Springs, Pennsylvania, 2013

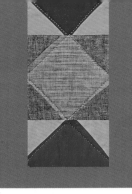

SQUARE IN A SQUARE

FINISHED QUILT: 72½″ × 96½″
FINISHED BLOCK: 8″ × 8″

Machine pieced and hand quilted by Sujata Shah, Chester Springs, Pennsylvania, 2013

Colors of India

Embroidery on
a traditional
Indian outfit

Kuba cloth from Kenya

YARDAGE REQUIREMENTS

Blocks:

- ⅔ yard each of 14 solid fabrics, 9⅓ yards total

Backing:

- 6 yards

Binding:

- ⅞ yard

Batting:

- Queen size or a piece 80″ × 104″

This quilt is a paint box of my memories of endless trips with my mom to the fabric shops overflowing with fabrics. As a little girl, I knew then, as much as I know now, that colors and textures ruled my world. Made with two-tone shot cottons and woven fabrics from India, this simple pattern was inspired by a pattern found in many objects, including a traditional embroidered outfit I wore as a young woman.

CUTTING INSTRUCTIONS

Blocks:
- From each solid, cut 2 strips 10″ × WOF*. Crosscut into 8 squares 10″ × 10″.

Backing:
- Cut 2 pieces 104″ × WOF.

Binding:
- Cut 10 strips 2½″ × WOF.

* WOF = width of fabric

MAKING THE BLOCKS

1. With right sides up, stack 4 squares 10″ × 10″ of 4 different colors. Make 27 stacks. (You will have 4 extra squares.)

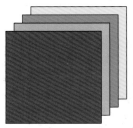

Stack.

2. Place a stack on the cutting mat, aligning the edges and corners of the squares. Slice through the layers with a straight line or gentle curve. Do not move the stack as you cut through the next corner; instead, rotate the mat. Make 4 slices.

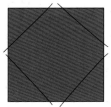

Slice.

> **TIP**
>
> Use the grid on the cutting mat to help eyeball the cuts through the corners of the stacks.

3. Lift the top diamond and place it at the bottom of the diamond stack. You have 4 corner triangles as a background and a diamond as the square in a square. The blocks are now in sewing order.

Slide the diamond.

4. Starting with the top layer, sew the upper right corner triangle to the corresponding edge of the diamond. Chain piece this corner for the rest of the diamonds.

5. Add the bottom right corner to each diamond, continuing to chain piece, followed by the final 2 corners in a clockwise order. Press the seams away from the center.

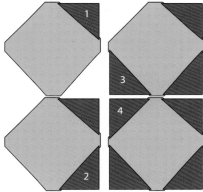

Add each corner in turn.

> **TIP**
>
> To avoid distorting the unsewn edges, do not press until all 4 sides of the background are pieced.

6. Repeat Steps 2–6 with the remaining stacks to make 108 blocks.

7. Trim the blocks to 8½″ × 8½″.

Trim.

ASSEMBLY

1. Arrange the blocks in 12 rows, with 9 blocks per row.

2. Sew the blocks together in rows. Press the seams in alternating directions from row to row.

3. Sew the rows together. Press the seams in one direction.

FINISHING

1. Sew the backing pieces together lengthwise.

2. Layer and baste together the backing, batting, and quilt top.

3. Machine or hand quilt.

4. Sew the binding strips together with diagonal seams. Bind the quilt.

Quilt assembly

 POSSIBILITIES

- Use pastels to make a baby quilt.

- Frame the blocks with sashing and cornerstones to create additional interest.

- Crosscut the block twice to make half-square triangles for a scrappy border or use them in a traditional block setting.

- Use heavyweight thread to add texture with organic quilting.

Bright blocks and organic quilting

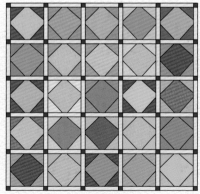

A variation on Tumbling Blocks

SUNSET

FINISHED QUILT: 45¾″ × 45¾″
FINISHED BLOCK: 8″ × 8″

Machine pieced and hand quilted by Sujata Shah, Chester Springs Pennsylvania, 2010

THE ROOT CONNECTION

Photo by Sujata Shah

There is something magical about the sky changing colors with the passing of every second at dusk. The last rays of sunshine paint the clouds, deep blue waves carry liquid gold to the shore, palm trees sway gently in the wind, and birds fly in a hurry to call it a day. Some of my favorite memories of childhood are of watching the sun go down on the Arabian Sea. To this day, I enjoy standing still as the sky darkens and the glow of amber and gold fades away into the dark.

YARDAGE REQUIREMENTS

Blocks:

- ¼ yard each of 13 blue solids
- ¼ yard each of 13 red and orange solids and prints

Side and corner triangles:

- 1 fat quarter each of 4 blue solids

Backing:

- 3 yards

Binding:

- ½ yard

Batting:

- Twin size or a piece 53″ × 53″

CUTTING INSTRUCTIONS

Blocks:

- From each blue fabric, cut 1 strip 7½″ × WOF*. Crosscut 4 squares 7½″ × 7½″.

- From each red or orange fabric, cut 1 strip 7½″ × WOF. Crosscut 4 squares 7½″ × 7½″.

Side and corner triangles:

- From each fat quarter, cut 1 square 12⅝″ × 12⅝″. Cut diagonally twice.

Backing:

- Cut 2 pieces 52″ × WOF.

Binding:

- Cut 5 strips 2½″ × WOF.

* WOF = width of fabric

MAKE THE BLOCKS

1. With right sides up, stack 4 squares 7½″ × 7½″: 2 squares of the same blue and 2 of the same red or orange.

2. Arrange the stack with the colors in alternating order. Make 26 stacks.

Stack.

3. Follow instructions from *Square in a Square*, Making the Blocks, Steps 2–5 (page 66). When slicing off the 4 corner triangles, make sure the diamond points are about ½″ wide.

4. Repeat Step 3 with the remaining stacks to make 104 blocks. (You will have 8 extra to allow for choice when placing the half-square triangles in the quilt.)

> **TIP**
>
> Make all the blocks before trimming them. This gives you flexibility with the shape and size of the triangles. While trimming, you can adjust the placement of the ruler to vary the triangle shapes as desired.

5. Trim the blocks to 5″ × 5″.

Trim.

6. Crosscut each block twice to make 4 half-square triangles for a total of 416.

Crosscut twice.

WAVE BLOCK ASSEMBLY

1. Place 16 half-square triangles together in 4 rows of 4 squares each, with the darker triangles on the left half of the block.

> **TIP**
>
> Shuffle the half-square triangles around to make a gradual transition from half-square triangles dominated with blue to the ones dominated with red and orange.

2. Sew the half-square triangles into 4 rows. Press the seams in alternating directions from row to row.

3. Sew together the rows. Press the seams in one direction.

4. Make 24 Wave blocks.

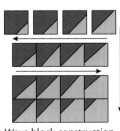

Wave block construction

QUILT ASSEMBLY

1. Sew together 4 Wave blocks with all the red/orange triangles toward the center to make a Sunset block. Press the seams open. Make 5.

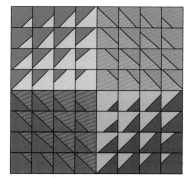

Sunset block

2. Sew side triangles to 2 adjoining sides of each remaining Wave block to make 4 pieced side triangles.

Pieced side triangle

3. Sew together 2 side triangles to make a corner triangle. Make 4.

Corner triangle

4. Assemble the quilt top in a diagonal setting. Sew together the pieces into diagonal rows. Press seams in alternating directions from row to row.

5. Sew together the rows. Press the seams in one direction.

FINISHING

1. Sew the backing pieces together lengthwise.

2. Layer and baste together the backing, batting, and quilt top.

3. Machine or hand quilt.

4. Sew the binding strips together with diagonal seams. Bind the quilt.

Quilt assembly

POSSIBILITIES

- Mix prints and solids containing a common color to make the half-square triangles disappear into the background fabric.

- Use stripes and plaids with solids to create additional texture and movement.

- Arrange all the blocks facing the same direction.

- Arrange 4 blocks with the dark half-square triangles toward the inside.

- Explore diagonal or straight setting of blocks alternating with a solid background.

- Set the blocks on point. Switch the dark and light sides of the blocks from row to row.

A variation of Birds in the Air

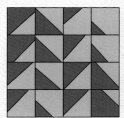 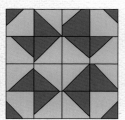  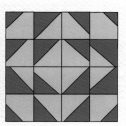

Additional block options

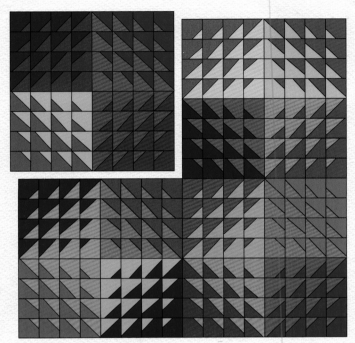

A variation of Storm at Sea

Golden City

ZIGZAG AMISH IMPRESSIONS

FINISHED QUILT: 42½″ × 42½″
FINISHED BLOCK: 3″ × 3″

Pieced and machine quilted by Sujata Shah, Chester Springs, Pennsylvania, 2010

The Moment

Quilts are wordless documents of personal and family history written in stitches. If this quilt could, it would tell you about my two sons' first summer in Pennsylvania. Thunder, lightning, and flooding were the stories of the day. The day had turned into the night. Drawn by the power of nature, the two brothers rushed out to the front porch to hear the sounds and feel the sensation of nature's fury. For them, the storm was nothing new, but for a mother watching her grown-up sons run outside and be in the moment was heartwarming.

YARDAGE REQUIREMENTS

Blocks:
- 1⅞ yards gray solid
- ⅜ yard each of at least 7 different solids

Backing:
- 3 yards

Binding:
- ½ yard

Batting:
- Twin size or a piece 50˝ × 50˝

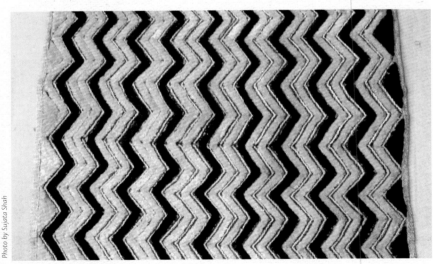

Kuba cloth from Kenya

CUTTING INSTRUCTIONS

Blocks:

- From the gray solid, cut 7 strips 9″ × WOF*. Crosscut each strip into 4 squares 9″ × 9″. (You will have 2 extra squares.)

- From each ⅜ yard, cut 1 strip 9″ × WOF. Crosscut each strip into 4 squares 9″ × 9″. (You will have 2 extra squares.)

Backing:

- Cut 2 pieces 50″ × WOF.

Binding:

- Cut 5 strips 2½″ × WOF.

WOF = width of fabric

MAKING THE BLOCKS

1. With right sides up, stack 4 squares 9″ × 9″: 2 of the same solid and 2 gray.

2. Arrange the stack with the colors in alternating order. Make 13 stacks.

Stack.

3. Follow instructions from *Square in a Square*, Making the Blocks, Steps 2–5 (page 66). When slicing off the 4 corner triangles, make sure the diamond points are about ½″ wide. The slice at each corner should be a slight curve.

4. Repeat Step 3 with the remaining stacks to make 49 blocks.

5. Trim the blocks to 7″ × 7″.

> **TIP**
>
> Skip Step 5; instead of trimming the squares, crosscut each twice (Step 6). Then fussy cut the resulting half-square triangles to get different sizes of triangles within the squares. Each half-square triangle must measure 3½″ × 3½″.
>
>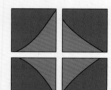
>
> Fussy-cut half-square triangles

6. Crosscut each block twice to make half-square triangles 3½″ × 3½″ for a total of 196. *Note:* Each square produces 4 half-square triangles. The triangles in each square vary in size.

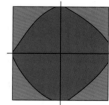

Crosscut twice.

ASSEMBLY

1. Following the quilt assembly diagram, place the half-square triangles in 14 rows with 14 per row. Play around with placement of colors and shapes to form zigzags.

2. Sew the blocks in rows. Press the seams in alternating directions from row to row.

3. Sew the rows together. Press the seams in one direction.

FINISHING

1. Sew the backing pieces together lengthwise.

2. Layer and baste together the backing, batting, and quilt top.

3. Machine or hand quilt.

4. Sew the binding strips together with diagonal seams. Bind the quilt.

⚡ TIP

Shuffle the half-square triangles for variations in the pattern. The same squares will make different zigzags in different spots. Mix them up or group large triangles together and small triangles together to create bold and drastic changes in the overall pattern.

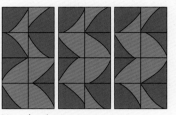

Vary the zigzag pattern.

Quilt assembly

POSSIBILITIES

- Group the half-square triangles by color.

- Combine prints and solids for a scrappy version.

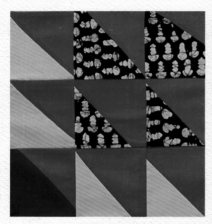

A variation on
Sunshine and Shadow

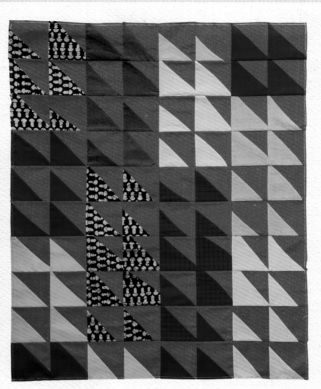

Child's Play, 36″ × 36″,
machine pieced and
machine quilted by Sujata
Shah, Chester Springs,
Pennsylvania, 2007

PEPPERMINT PINWHEELS

FINISHED QUILT: 64½″ × 64½″

FINISHED BLOCK: 16″ × 16″

Machine pieced and hand quilted by Sujata Shah, Chester Springs, Pennsylvania, 2010

Stone carvings on a temple wall in India

Photo by Sujata Shah

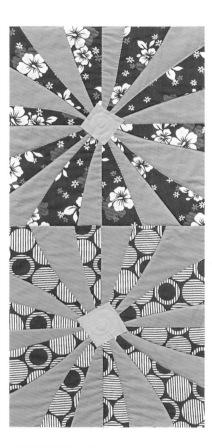

Appliqué pillow cover from Pakistan

From a distance, hand-carved flowers look symmetrical, but up close, each petal is a different shape and size. I love that about anything handmade. It has the thumbprint of the maker. We all know that humans can achieve perfection maybe once, but only machines can reproduce the same thing twice.

The ralli pillowcase from Pakistan has a motif with flowers in the four corners. Up close, each one has a personality of its own. Missing petals, off-centered placement, and varying size of the appliqué all add the mark of the maker.

YARDAGE REQUIREMENTS

Blocks:

- 3½ yards of solid green for background
- ⅜ yard each of 16 red-and-white prints for flowers

Flower centers:

- ¼ yard each of light green, red, and white solids

Backing:

- 4⅛ yards

Binding:

- ⅝ yard

Batting:

- Twin size or a piece 72″ × 72″

CUTTING INSTRUCTIONS

Blocks:

- From the solid green, cut 11 strips 11″ × WOF*. Crosscut each strip to make 3 squares 11″ × 11″ for a total of 32.

- From each of the 16 red-and-white fabrics, cut 1 strip 11″ × WOF. Crosscut to make 2 squares 11″ × 11″ for a total of 32.

Backing:

- Cut 2 pieces 72″ × WOF.

Binding:

- Cut 7 strips 2½″ × WOF.

WOF = width of fabric

MAKING THE BLOCKS

1. With right sides up, stack 4 squares 11″ × 11″: 2 of the same print and 2 green.

2. Arrange the stack with the colors in alternating order. Make 16 stacks.

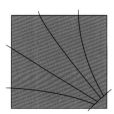

Stack.

3. Place a stack on the cutting mat, aligning the edges and corners of the squares. Trim off diagonally about an inch from the lower right corner. This helps to minimize bunching of seams.

4. Do not move the stack. Slice through all 4 layers, 4 times as shown. Start with the 2 center cuts.

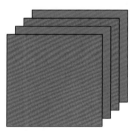

Slice.

5. Slide the top petals (pieces 2 and 4) to the bottom of their corresponding places. The block pieces are now in the correct sewing order.

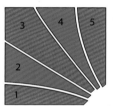

Slide alternating petals.

6. Start sewing from the left side. Chain piece Petal 2 to Petal 1 for all 4 layers. Continue adding Petals 3, 4, and 5. Press the seams toward Petal 1.

 TIP

> To avoid distorting the unsewn edges, do not press until all the petals are pieced to the background.

7. Trim the petal blocks to 8½″ × 8½″.

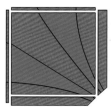

Trim.

8. Piece together 4 blocks to make a Peppermint Pinwheel block 16½″ × 16½″. Press the seam allowances in the direction of the arrows.

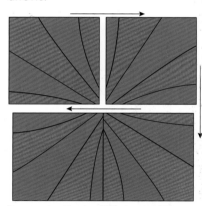

Peppermint Pinwheel block assembly

9. Repeat Steps 3–8 with the remaining stacks to make 16 Peppermint Pinwheel blocks.

10. Cut squares from craft or freezer paper to determine your preferred size for the block centers.

11. Cut the centers from the ¼ yard of solids. If hand appliquéing, add a seam allowance to each center shape.

12. Machine or hand appliqué the squares onto the center of the blocks.

ASSEMBLY

1. Arrange the 16 blocks in 4 rows, with 4 blocks per row.

2. Sew together each row. Press the seams in alternating directions from row to row.

3. Sew the rows together. Press the seams in one direction.

FINISHING

1. Sew the backing pieces together lengthwise.

2. Layer and baste together the backing, batting, and quilt top.

3. Machine or hand quilt.

4. Sew the binding strips together with diagonal seams. Bind the quilt.

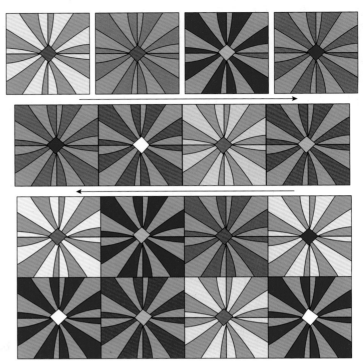

Quilt assembly

 POSSIBILITIES

- Make a quilt with multiple colors.

- In Making the Blocks, Step 1 (page 81), stack 5 different squares.

- Use the petal blocks individually as Fan blocks.

- Piece or appliqué the centers in varying sizes and shapes.

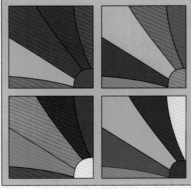

A variation of Grandmother's Fan

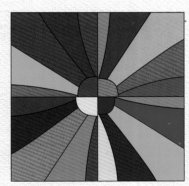

A variation of Rising Sun

ENDLESS MOUNTAINS

FINISHED QUILT: 60″ × 90½″ *(Your quilt size may vary depending on the number of triangles cut per strip.)*

FINISHED STRIP: 5″ × 15″

Pieced by Sujata Shah; machine quilted by Barbara Jackson, Redmond, Washington, 2013

Block print fabric from India

Carved gourd from Africa

Folk artists around the world use similar design elements in their art. Triangles in a block print from India reflect the mountain ranges at the edge of the desert. Triangles on a carved gourd from Africa reflect the peaks of an endless mountain range.

YARDAGE REQUIREMENTS

Triangle strips:
- ¼ yard each of 18 light fabrics
- ¼ yard each of 18 dark fabrics

Backing:
- 5⅝ yards

Binding:
- ¾ yard

Batting:
- Queen size or a piece 68″ × 98″

CUTTING INSTRUCTIONS

Triangle strips:

- From each light fabric, cut 1 strip 6″ × WOF*. Cut each strip in half lengthwise to yield 2 strips 6″ × approximately 20″.

- From each dark fabric, cut 1 strip 6″ × WOF. Cut each strip in half lengthwise to yield 2 strips 6″ × approximately 20″.

Backing:

- Cut 2 pieces 98″ × WOF.

Binding:

- Cut 9 strips 2½″ × WOF.

* WOF = width of fabric

MAKING THE TRIANGLE STRIPS

1. With right sides up, stack 4 strips 6″ × approximately 20″: 2 of the same dark and 2 of the same light.

2. Arrange the stack with the values in alternating order. Make 18 stacks.

Stack.

3. Pace a stack on the cutting mat, aligning the edges and corners of the squares. Freehand cut 6 or 7 times to create 5 or 6 triangles.

Slice.

TIP

Experiment with cutting triangles before starting this quilt. The quilt will look different depending on the angle of the cut and the number of triangles per strip. Practice on a paper template to determine the triangle size and angles that fit on the strip. Wide angles will yield fewer triangles. To make a paper template, cut the strip of paper to the size specified. With a marker, draw the number of desired triangles. They do not have to all be the same size or have perfect points. Use your "eyeballing" skills.

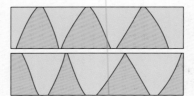

Strips made with odd number of triangles yield 2 inverted sets of strips.

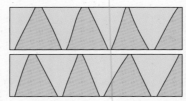

Strips made with even number of triangles yield triangles pointing the same way.

Triangles with tops cut off

4. Slide alternating patches of triangles to the bottom of the stack.

Slide.

5. Starting from the left, chain piece the first 2 triangles of all 4 layers. Continue chain piecing, adding the next triangle to the pieced section, until all triangles are sewn into a strip. Press seams to the dark fabric. Make 4 strips.

 TIP

> To avoid distorting the unsewn edges, do not press until all the triangles are sewn into each strip.

6. Repeat Steps 3–5 with the remaining stacks to make 72 triangle strips. Keep the strips together in their original stacks.

7. Trim each strip to 5½˝ × varied lengths. Trim the ends to be at 90°.

8. In each stack, make sure that all the dark triangles point in the same direction. If not, flip strips 180° so that they do.

Flip strip on right to have all dark triangles pointing up.

9. Sew identical strips end to end.

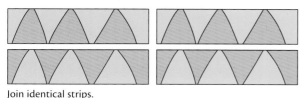

Join identical strips.

10. Again, make sure that all the dark triangles point in the same direction. With right sides up, align and overlap the 2 strips to form a continuous triangle pattern.

Two strips with overlapping edges to make a triangle

11. Trim the overlapped section at 90°. Sew together the 2 strips.

12. Trim the strip to 5½˝ × 60˝.

Join and trim.

13. Repeat Steps 8–12 for all the stacks of strips to make 18 triangle rows.

ASSEMBLY

Sew together the triangle rows along their long edges. Press the seams in one direction.

TIP

Alternate the sewing direction with each strip to avoid stretching the fabric too much in one direction. This will help keep the top straight.

FINISHING

1. Sew the backing pieces together lengthwise.

2. Layer and baste together the backing, batting, and quilt top.

3. Machine or hand quilt.

4. Sew the binding strips together with diagonal seams. Bind the quilt.

Quilt assembly

- Piece strips into blocks instead of rows to make zigzag blocks.

- Have all the triangles facing in the same direction for mountain blocks.

- Make zigzag rows by pairing the fabric strips in this manner:

  1 and 2, 2 and 3, 3 and 4, …
  up to 16 and 17, 17 and 18

Work with one combination at a time, following the general directions for Making the Triangle Strips (page 85).

Scrappy Triangles, 28½″ × 26½″, machine pieced and quilted by Dorothy (Sally) LeBoeuf, Edmonds, Washington, 2011

Zigzag blocks

Mountain blocks

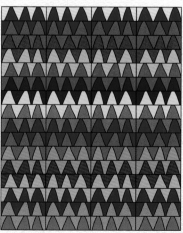

Zigzag rows

Hawaiian Triangles, 51½" × 77",
machine pieced and quilted
by Dorothy (Sally) LeBoeuf,
Edmonds, Washington, 2011

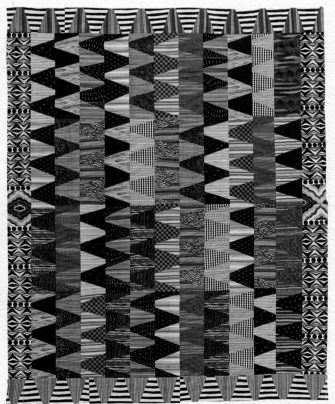

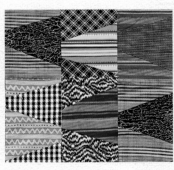

Double Helix, 62" × 84",
machine pieced and quilted
by Mary Ramsey Keasler,
Cleveland, Tennessee, 2013

WINTER

FINISHED QUILT: 42½" × 49½"
FINISHED BLOCK: 7" × 7"

Machine pieced and machine quilted by Sujata Shah, Chester Springs, Pennsylvania, 2010

THE ROOT CONNECTION

Lancaster County farmland

For someone who loves gardening and creating with colors, the snowy days of winter can be harsh. Dreaming of spring and summer gardens, I made a quilt only to discover that the gray and cold days had also affected my color choices. Soft gray and white tones reflect the cold winter days during my first year in Pennsylvania.

YARDAGE REQUIREMENTS

Blocks:

- ⅓ yard each of 11 assorted light, medium, and dark values in gray and earth tones

Backing:

- 3 yards

Binding:

- ½ yard

Batting:

- Twin size or a piece 50″ × 57″

Leaf motif on carved gourd from Africa

Photo by Sujata Shah

CUTTING INSTRUCTIONS

Blocks:

- From each fabric, cut 1 strip 9″ × WOF*. Crosscut 4 squares 9″ × 9″ for a total of 44 squares.

Backing:

- Cut 2 pieces 50″ × WOF.

Binding:

- Cut 5 strips 2½″ × WOF.

WOF = width of fabric

MAKING THE BLOCKS

1. With right sides up, stack 4 contrasting squares 9″ × 9″. Make 11 stacks.

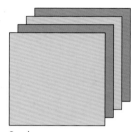

Stack.

2. Place the stack on the cutting mat, aligning the edges and corners of the squares. Slice the right edge of the leaf all through the stack. Slide the ruler gently while cutting with a rotary cutter to get a gentle curve.

3. Slice the left edge of the leaf.

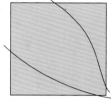

Slice.

 TIP

Slicing the right edge first helps to keep the stack in place.

 TIP

With each stack, you may end up with a different thickness of the leaves. That's the beauty of organic cutting and piecing. Do not stress if the leaves are irregular and asymmetrical.

4. Slide the leaf from the top to the bottom of the stack. The blocks are now in sewing order.

Slide.

5. With right sides together, matching the points, sew the leaf to the left background piece. Chain piece the remaining leaves in the stack to the left-side background pieces.

 TIP

To avoid distorting the unsewn edges, do not press until both sides of the background are pieced.

6. Chain piece the right side of the background to the left half of the block in the same order. Press the seams away from the center.

7. Repeat Steps 2–6 with the remaining stacks for a total of 42 blocks. You will have 2 extra.

8. Trim the blocks to 7½″ × 7½″.

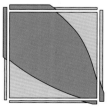

Trim.

ASSEMBLY

1. Arrange the blocks in 7 horizontal rows, each containing 6 blocks.

2. Sew the blocks in rows. Press the seams in alternating directions from row to row.

3. Sew the rows together. Press the seams in one direction.

FINISHING

1. Sew the backing pieces together lengthwise.

2. Layer and baste together the backing, batting, and quilt top.

3. Machine or hand quilt.

4. Sew the binding strips together with diagonal seams. Bind the quilt.

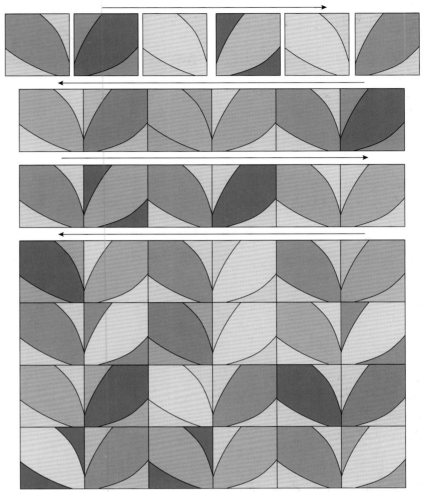

Quilt assembly

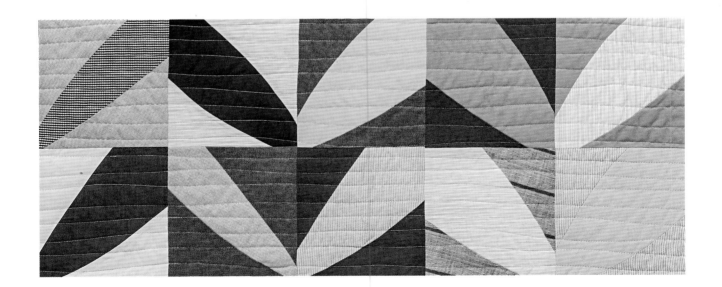

POSSIBILITIES

- Try large prints or predominantly two-color printed fabrics.

- Choose 2 colors and make a Robbing Peter to Pay Paul version of the quilt to create positive and negative space in the quilt.

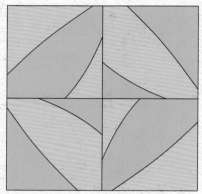

A variation of Robbing Peter to Pay Paul

Leaf, 60½″ × 74½″, machine pieced and quilted by Dorothy (Sally) LeBoeuf, Edmonds, Washington, 2011

ABOUT THE AUTHOR

Photo by Kavita Shah

Sujata Shah, a graphic designer and textile lover, is originally from Mumbai, India. The mother of three grown children, she lives with her husband in Chester Springs, Pennsylvania.

She is an award-winning quilter and has designed quilt patterns under the name Rangoli Designs. Her teaching experiences include workshops inspired by the quilts of Gee's Bend in the Seattle area and in Philadelphia.

Sujata finds inspiration from the textures and imperfections of handmade objects such as patchwork, embroidered and woven textiles of India, mud cloth, adire cloth, and starch-resist cloths of Africa. Her exposure to different cultures has helped develop her distinctive style of quilts, which blends utilitarian and traditional quilts in an exciting way.

Great Titles *from* C&T PUBLISHING

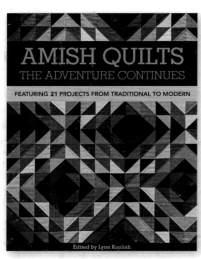

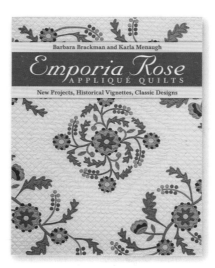

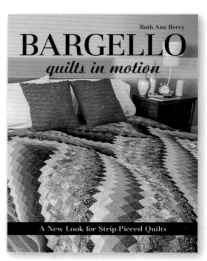

Available at your local retailer or **ctpub.com** *or* **800-284-1114**

For a list of other fine books from C&T Publishing, visit our website to view our catalog online.

C&T PUBLISHING, INC.
P.O. Box 1456
Lafayette, CA 94549
800-284-1114

Email: ctinfo@ctpub.com
Website: ctpub.com

C&T Publishing's professional photography services are now available to the public. Visit us at ctmediaservices.com.

Tips and Techniques can be found at ctpub.com > Consumer Resources > Quiltmaking Basics: Tips & Techniques for Quiltmaking & More

For quilting supplies:

COTTON PATCH
1025 Brown Ave.
Lafayette, CA 94549
Store: 925-284-1177
Mail order: 925-283-7883

Email: CottonPa@aol.com
Website: quiltusa.com

Note: Fabrics shown may not be currently available, as fabric manufacturers keep most fabrics in print for only a short time.